PLAGUE and
PESTILENCE

Margrete Lamond was born in Norway and migrated to Australia with her family at the age of eight. She started producing stories as soon as she could write, and was first published when she was only 16. After working on the staff of a children's magazine she moved to the country, and she now divides her time between writing (mostly plays and non-fiction), sole parenting, studying, reading, gardening, horse riding and flamenco dancing.

Margrete's earlier book in the True Stories series is *Going for It!: Success Stories of Women in Sport*.

Margrete Lamond

PLAGUE and PESTILENCE

deadly diseases that changed the world

A LITTLE
ARK
BOOK

ALLEN & UNWIN

First published in 1994.
This edition first published 1997.
A Little Ark Book.
Allen & Unwin Pty Ltd
Distributed in the U.S.A. by
Independent Publishers Group,
814 North Franklin Street,
Chicago, IL. 60610,
Phone 312 337 0747,
Fax 312 337 5985,
Internet: ipgbook@mcs.com
Distributed in Canada by
McClelland & Stewart,
481 University Avenue,
Suite 900,
Toronto, O.N. M5G 2E9,
Phone 416 1114,
Fax 416 598 4002

10 9 8 7 6 5 4 3 2 1

ISBN 1 86448 456 X

Picture credits
Photos of Ebola patients supplied by Sygma/Austral International
(photographer for nun in coffin, P. Robert); all other photos supplied by
Coo-ee Historical Picture Library

Thanks to Catherine O'Rourke for photo research

Cover design by Sandra Nobes
Typeset by Midland Typesetters
Printed by McPherson's Printing Group

Contents

Introduction

London, summer 1665

"Bring out yer dead! Bring out yer dead!"

The death-cart creaks.

Stumbling ahead, the bellman rouses a night-watchman where he dozes outside a house. The door is barred, and on it a cross has been painted. Underneath are the words *'GOD HELP OUR SOULS!'*

They force open the door and the stench of death fills the night air – sickly, sweet and thick. A family of bodies is hauled out. Their limbs, limp and soggy, dangle and swing from the sides of the cart.

"Bring out yer dead!"

Further on, a woman shrieks as her dead child is tossed on top of the load. The cart blunders on, heavier and slower with each stop. At last all is quiet in the alley…except for the cries and moans coming from behind barred doors and windows – the sound of a city in the grip of *bubonic plague.*

Bubonic plague is an epidemic disease which comes on suddenly, and which can kill half of those it infects. It starts with headaches, shivering, giddiness and vomiting, followed by pains in the back, arms and legs. Before long the tell-tale signs begin to appear – black blotches caused by bleeding under the skin, which bloom like 'rings of roses' around the neck and wrists and under the arms.

Then come the most characteristic signs of bubonic plague – painful swellings, or buboes, in the groin and armpits. Bubonic plague is named after these lumps. As the patient gets worse, there is fever, sleeplessness and delirium. In the *pneumonic* form of plague, the patient coughs and spits up blood. If untreated, the patient is likely to die in less than four days from the pneumonic form, and within 24 hours from the lethal *septicaemic* variety.

For the people of London in 1665, plague meant fear, despair, and even madness. They struggled to find answers to seemingly impossible questions. Where did it come from? Why? How could they protect themselves? Was there a cure?

Although this particular epidemic killed an estimated 7000 people every week, it was not an unusual event. Historic records show that plagues and epidemics had been affecting people for thousands of years, killing millions upon millions worldwide. Epidemics have been more deadly than all the wars of history combined.

> **Epidemics have been more deadly than all the wars of history combined.**

New diseases are still being discovered. Mysterious fevers have flared in Africa and South America. Illnesses believed to have disappeared are returning, stronger and tougher than before. Bugs and germs have become resistant to the medicines that once killed them.

This book will outline the great plagues and epidemics of history. It will describe the symptoms. It will look into the side-effects. It will explore results. It will even reveal how history itself was shaped and altered by the power of the mighty germ!

What Was It?
The Plague of Athens

It was early summer, and the great city-state of Athens had been at war with Sparta for a year. Large enemy armies were camped throughout the countryside north of Athens, and thousands of country people had fled to the safety of its mighty walls. Makeshift shelters filled every available space along streets, in public squares and even in temples, and the refugees living in them sweltered under the merciless blaze of the summer sun.

It was a recipe for disaster – crowding, hot weather, hunger, dirt and war. Yet, when sickness struck, no one was prepared.

Starting near the harbor, plague was rampaging throughout the crowded city before the citizens had time to realize it. People infected each other so quickly that whole families 'died like sheep...in wild disorder'.

It started with a severe headache and red eyes, plus a sore tongue and throat. Sneezing, hoarseness and coughs soon followed; then intense vomiting, diarrhea, and an unbearable thirst. Then came delirium: the patients' minds became confused and they began seeing visions, raving wildly and throwing themselves about.

Bodies of the dead and dying lay heaped, one upon the other, in homes, on streets, in the temples. People staggered from their houses only to collapse in the dust, rolling and twisting in agony. Desperate with thirst, they dragged themselves to the public fountains, only to find their way blocked by the bodies of those who had died without reaching the water they craved.

Stunned by the horror around them, people gave up mourning their dead. Corpses of loved ones were tossed onto other people's funeral pyres.

'No pestilence of such extent or...so destructive of human lives is on record anywhere,' wrote Thucydides, an historian who survived the plague. 'It carried off all without distinction.'

The city's doctors were helpless: they had no remedies, and nothing they did was of any use.

For a quarter of the population, death came seven to nine days after their first headache began. Those who survived went on to suffer severe diarrhea and weakness. Their bodies would become covered in reddish spots, some of which turned into ulcers. Many ended up blind, while others permanently lost their memory.

Many ended up blind, while others permanently lost their memory.

The Plague of Athens raged for three years, but Athenians never discovered the cause of the disease. Modern *epidemiologists* – those who study epidemics – have made careful studies of Thucydides' descriptions of the plague. Some believe the Plague of Athens was bubonic plague. Others claim it was either cholera, typhus or smallpox.

1 Rumor and Superstition

Thinkers through the ages have always been fascinated by origins: the origin of human beings, the origin of life, the origin of the universe, the origin of disease.

Fact or theory?

Ancient thinkers came to some mistaken conclusions about the origins of things. The following, for example, were once considered absolute fact: insects are created from bamboo in humid weather (ancient China); insects come from sweat (ancient India); life originates from ooze and slime, body-lice come from meat, and fleas come from rotting compost (ancient Greece); wasps come from dead horses, beetles from dead donkeys, and bees from the corpses of young bulls (ancient Rome).

> A rumour went around that taking rocks out of the sea...had caused the epidemic.

These 'facts' fitted with what people saw, but we now know they are incorrect. In the same way, people came up with some odd beliefs about the causes of deadly disease.

Rumors...

In Siam (modern Thailand) in the early 1800s, people blamed the outbreak of cholera – a savage form of diarrhea – on landscaping done in the royal gardens.

A rumor went around that taking rocks out of the sea to build an artificial mountain for the king had caused the epidemic.

...And wild stories

The bubonic plague – or Black Death – of the 1300s was one of the most written-about plagues of the past. Before the plague reached Europe in 1345, there were reports from the Middle East and continental Asia about sheets of fire mixed with hailstones that were killing whole populations. Other reports described how a 'vast rain of fire' had burned up all people, animals, rocks, vegetation, villages and towns. People believed that 'foul blasts of wind' from these fires were carrying the infection towards Europe.

Some stories claimed that an earthquake had released foul, disease-causing fumes from deep inside the earth. Yet others explained how a struggle between certain planets and the ocean had made the waters rise and caused fish to die – and these dead fish had contaminated the air, thereby causing the Black Death.

After much research and argument, a group of medieval French doctors finally released their 'official version'. They said bubonic

DID YOU KNOW?
In fourteenth-century Europe, bubonic plague was known as 'The Great Pestilence' and 'The Great Mortality'. Muslims called it 'The Plague of the Kindred', 'The Great Destruction' and 'The Year of the Annihilation'.

11

plague was caused by a particular arrangement of the planets Saturn, Jupiter and Mars, which happened on 20 March 1345.

None the wiser

After the 1300s, bubonic plague kept returning to Europe, but doctors didn't become any the wiser as to its cause. In the Great Plague of London in 1665, people had ideas as strange as those of 300 years earlier. They thought that the poisonous breath of an infected person would kill a bird. And if a sick person breathed on a cold pane of glass, the condensation that formed would be full of 'strange, monstrous and frightful shapes, such as dragons, snakes, serpents and devils, horrible to behold'.

'A touch of the flu –'

In the 1800s and 1900s there were long and sometimes fiery discussions among medical people over the cause of influenza. Some declared it was caused by the weather, while others blamed earthquakes or volcanoes. Most decided it arose from poisons in the air called *miasmas*. Very few believed that flu was transmitted by people.

In 1918, during the world's worst influenza epidemic, one eminent American doctor decided that influenza was caused by 'small amounts of a depressing, highly irritating high-density gas, present

> **DID YOU KNOW?**
>
> 'Influenza' is an Italian word meaning 'the influence'. It was first used during an epidemic in 1504, because the Italians believed their sickness was due to the influence of the planets.

in the atmosphere, especially at night'. Others, equally respected, declared that the flu was caused by 'nakedness, dust, dirty pajamas, open windows, closed windows, old books'.

many people blamed the war for the disease

This flu pandemic – or worldwide epidemic – occurred during World War I and many people blamed the war for the disease. They said it was nature's way of punishing everyone for allowing this dreadful conflict. Another theory was that the enemy was using germ warfare.

DID YOU KNOW?
The 1918–19 flu pandemic killed 21 million people.

Poisonous mists

For many centuries, the most popular explanation for the cause of disease was *miasmas*, as mentioned above. Miasmas might be released from stagnant water in lakes and ponds. They might come from the stench of unburied corpses – particularly those left lying on battlefields. They might be caused by strange weather patterns. Shooting stars, comets and meteorites were thought to leave trails of 'noxious mist' behind them.

Explaining the cause of the bubonic plague in the fourteenth century, an Arab writer said, 'the wind transmitted the stench of the cadavers across the world. When this empoisoned blast dwelt on a city...or some region, it struck with death both men and beasts in the same instant.'

A 'pestilential miasma' was supposedly visible, looking like mist or smoke. According to the theory, it would ooze across the countryside, clinging to towns, buildings, clothes, bedding, animal fur and would be absorbed into people's bodies through their skin.

Swamp fever

Malaria is an infection causing high fevers, severe chills and heavy sweating. It is caused by a parasite which is carried by the *Anopheles* mosquito. People infected with the parasite can have bouts of malaria again and again throughout their lives. It was once called 'swamp fever' because it was believed to come from chemical poisons – or miasmas – which emanated from swamps.

> **DID YOU KNOW?**
> The name 'malaria' means 'bad air'. Other names given to malaria were 'marsh fever', 'river fever', and 'the ague'.

Europeans discovered malaria in a big way during the nineteenth century, when they started settling in the tropical countries of Africa, South America and South-east Asia. Unaware of the part played by mosquitoes in these recurring swamp fevers, they looked around for other possible causes.

Sir Richard Burton was an English explorer who became famous for being the first white person to discover Lake Tanganyika in southern Africa. He believed malaria fevers came from sleeping outside on bright, moonlit nights. Others thought it was due to

> **Sir Richard Burton...believed malaria fevers came from sleeping outside on bright, moonlit nights.**

alcoholism, and gave malaria the nickname 'whiskeyitis'. There were even theories attributing the fevers to the fierce rays of the tropical sun.

Gifts of the gods

In some South-east Asian countries, folklore explains how illnesses like cholera, leprosy or plague were inflicted by demons, ghosts, dragons or sorcerers. In Bali, people believed cholera was one of the deadly instruments of a warlike magician. Bubonic plague was the ghastly invention of a witch, while leprosy – a disease of the skin and nerves – was a curse from the gods. Smallpox, however, was considered a divine gift.

Islamic countries believed that bubonic plague was inflicted by evil *jinn* – but these *jinn* were actually the agents of God. Because God could do no evil, Muslims considered the 'Great Destruction' to be a mercy and a blessing.

Guilt and punishment

In Christian Europe, however, the plague was believed to be divine punishment. People believed 'the pestilence' was sent by God to punish wrong-doers. Punishable misdeeds included

> People believed 'the pestilence' was sent by God

wearing newfangled women's fashions, drunkenness and swearing, not going to church, abandoning the Catholic faith, and not believing in God.

If sickness was a punishment – so the logic went – then those who became sick were obviously sinners. The more dreadful the disease, the more serious the sins. Because the Black Death was the most widespread and ghastly natural disaster Europe had ever experienced, everyone felt guilty.

Better than nothing

From creeping mists to vengeful gods, people of the past found little comfort, and much to fear, in their explanations for disease. But no matter how alarming or doubtful their theories, a frightening answer was better than no answer at all. During times of deadly disease, one of the great horrors lies in not knowing *why*, *where* or *how*.

What Is It?
Cholera

Bangkok, Siam, 1820

Night after night, as the moon slowly grows, cannons boom throughout the city. The Palace halls echo with the trills of sacred Buddhist chants, while monks in yellow robes carry the Emerald Buddha and other holy objects in procession around the walls of the city. King Rama II has ordered all work to be suspended. The markets are closed, palace servants have been sent home, convicts have been released from prison, and captive animals have been freed to return to the jungle.

But behind the prayers and processions, behind the chanting, the incense and the charity, there is fear. People are dying by the thousands, and everyone is frantic. Cholera – unknown and deadly – has struck the kingdom of Siam.

We now know that chlorine discourages it. Antibiotics can alleviate it. Salts and lots of water repair its damaging effects. Untreated, however, cholera is deadly. It can sweep through a city in days, and up to 50 per cent of victims are likely to die. Along with loss of appetite, a person infected with cholera bacteria first feels a swelling of the stomach. Then he or she becomes giddy and may collapse. Hands and feet become clammy and cold.

The next onslaught of symptoms is sudden. Violent stomach spasms are followed by intense vomiting and diarrhea – typically of a pale liquid which looks like rice-water. There is heavy sweating and fever.

As the body loses more and more fluids, it begins to shrivel. Agonizing cramps attack arm and leg muscles, contorting

17

and crumpling them into excruciating knots. Blood capillaries burst, so that the skin turns black and blue. The stomach becomes hollow and caved in, the eyes sunken; a wild and terrified expression settles on the suddenly gaunt features.

> **As the body loses more and more fluids, it begins to shrivel.**

Breathing is labored, the pulse drops, and death from severe dehydration follows – sometimes after a few hours, sometimes after days of torment.

An ancient native of Bengal, India, the cholera germ is a comma-shaped water bacteria called *Vibrio cholerae*. Humans are its only carriers and it is passed from person to person through water or food contaminated by infected human feces.

For thousands of years, cholera was known only in India. Epidemics in that country often happened during mass pilgrimages to holy spots along the River Ganges, when hundreds of thousands of people were crowded together with no clean water.

In 1817 a series of severe outbreaks broke this pattern. Three major pandemics, each one more serious and far-reaching than the last, spread to nearly every part of the globe. Cholera killed millions of people throughout the nineteenth century. Severe outbreaks still occur.

Cholera is often a disease of the poor. People who have to scoop their drinking water from rivers into which others have poured their filth are most likely to catch it; so are slum-dwellers, refugees, and victims of natural disasters.

Modern hygiene has banished this menace from most peoples' experience. However, where sanitation breaks down, or where it does not exist, the threat of cholera remains.

2 Warding Off the Enemy

Cholera was a mystery to the Siamese. They didn't know where it came from or how to cure it. The best they could do was attempt to prevent it spreading. With no scientific knowledge about the disease, however, they had to rely on magic and religion – scaring it away with cannon fire, warding it off with holy chants, inviting the return of peace and health with good deeds and pure living.

Magic or medicine?

Before the advent of modern science, people often confused magic with medicine. They practiced a wide variety of customs in order to ward off disease: wearing red, ringing church bells, hanging

(**people often confused magic with medicine**)

toads around their necks, killing cats and dogs, whipping themselves, or placing thorn bushes across roads to keep disease-demons away. These health measures either worked by sheer fluke, or else made no difference at all. Others even made matters worse.

Herbs and spice and all things nice...

'*Take black pepper, red and white sandalwood, rose petals, camphor and some Armenian clay; grind them up fine; pound, shake and sift them with rosewater over a period of a week; form into an 'apple' with rosewater and gum arabic...'*

This recipe for 'smelling-apples' was prescribed by the University of Paris in the fourteenth century. Carrying your 'apple' and sniffing it from time to time was supposed to protect you against bubonic plague.

Smells were once considered an important part of disease prevention. In ancient Greece, a famous doctor called Hippocrates taught that sweet aromas created a shield against disease-bearing miasmas in the air.

In Middle Eastern countries, musk – a key ingredient of perfume – was in high demand during times of plague. Perfumes made of lemon, rose or violet were supposed to be particularly beneficial.

In Europe, people carried 'posies' made up of fragrant flowers and herbs such as lavender, rosemary and sweet marjoram. They were used not only to cover the stench of death and decay, but also to protect the carriers from the plague. Sweet scents were not the only useful ones. Another Middle Eastern belief declared that the stink of excreta and vile-smelling smoke was also effective, the theory being that miasmas could compete with neither sweet nor foul air.

An onion a day

Nothing was considered so healthful as vinegar. From London to Cairo, people washed in it, drank it, soaked their clothes in it, breathed through cloths that had been wetted with it, splashed it around sickrooms and even inhaled it.

The sourness of lemons, the astringence of

pomegranates, and the pungence of raw onions were thought to be wholesome too. People in Arab countries believed that a pickled onion before breakfast every day was certain to ward off plague.

Purification by fire

In Athens in 430 B.C., Hippocrates advised people to light fires throughout the city to cleanse the air. In London in 1665, coal fires were kept burning in the streets and inside houses all summer long, no matter how hot the weather. In the mid-1300s, Pope Clement VI was ordered by his doctor to spend the entire summer sitting alone in his apartment between two blazing fires.

Fire didn't help the ancient Athenians, but it worked for the Pope. While people died of bubonic plague by the thousands throughout Europe, Clement VI remained well.

Fires were supposed to protect people against miasmas. Dry, crackling heat supposedly purified the atmosphere, dissipating 'noxious fumes' and burning up the 'venomous creatures' which bred in the air.

However, the reason for Pope Clement's continued health was more likely due to the fact that the plague-bearing fleas couldn't stand the heat of his apartments.

Fumigants and disinfectants

Typhus fever thrives in dirty, crowded conditions. It is spread by lice and was the curse of the British navy in the 1800s and 1900s.

DID YOU KNOW?
Typhus is also called 'jail fever', 'spotted fever' and 'shipboard fever'.

Unaware of the insect connection, a navy doctor of the early 1880s recommended thorough disinfection of ships' sleeping quarters as a way of beating the disease. He believed that infection stuck to such things as wooden beams and furniture, as well as to clothes and people. Smoke and fumes were also used to drive away infection. People burnt tobacco, pitch, tar, gunpowder and charcoal, and set out containers of camphorated vinegar.

Similar measures – such as burning perfumes, incense, rosin and sulphur in infected rooms, followed by an explosion of gunpowder to blast away the last dregs of miasma – were used to combat everything from bubonic plague to cholera.

DID YOU KNOW?
Tobacco was regarded as an especially good weapon against disease, so that people sometimes smoked to stay healthy!

Prayers and processions

Faces smeared with tears and ashes, bodies clothed in sackcloth, feet bare and bleeding, hundreds of people wandered the streets holding up candles, crucifixes and holy relics. These processions – sometimes of as many as 2000 – wound their way up and down the streets of European cities. Praying and wailing, the participants cried out to God and his saints for mercy. Some wore heavy ropes around their necks. Others lashed at themselves with whips.

Christians of the fourteenth century believed it was their own sins which had brought the wrath of God – and the plague – upon them. They hoped that taking part in religious processions and ceremonies, or punishing themselves in various ways, would please God and encourage him to take the plague away.

> the result was to spread disease rather than stop it

These gatherings often had the opposite effect. As thousands of people – some of them infected – crowded together in city streets, the result was to spread disease rather than stop it.

Ritual dances

The sacred mask of the Balinese *rangda* is a gruesome spectacle. It is smeared with blood and dripping entrails, with matted hair, a huge tongue hanging loose and bloodshot, bulging eyes. This shows both the effects of death by plague, and the grotesque witch believed to be the cause of it.

The *rangda* is the center of a dance-drama, the *Calon Arang*, which is performed in Balinese temples. Showing all aspects of epidemics – from the wild arrival of the witch and terrified flight of victims, to the gruesome distortions of death – the *Calon Arang* is believed to control epidemic disease.

Quarantine

In West Africa, separation of the sick from the healthy was practiced long before European countries made it a rule. When anyone came down with smallpox, a special hut was built for them outside the village, where they could stay until they died or got better. Someone who had already recovered from smallpox would be sent to look after them.

The European idea of *quarantine* was born in Italy when bubonic plague arrived by sea in 1348. When help from God did not come, Archbishop Giovanni Visconti of Milan took drastic measures. He ordered that members of the first three households showing signs of plague be bricked into their homes. Old and young, masters and servants, were all entombed along with the dying and the dead.

Old and young, masters and servants, were all entombed

While Milan entombed the sick, the port of Venice screened all visitors by keeping them isolated on an island for 40 days. If they showed no signs of plague after that time, they were allowed into the city. The rest of Europe soon followed Italy's example and by the fifteenth century, the quarantining of ships was standard practice in all European ports. Quarantine is still practiced by many countries today – mostly to protect local agriculture or wildlife.

For the common good

Quarantining is meant to protect the public at large. However, some early quarantine procedures were

needlessly harsh.
Families were
barred in their
homes or, worse

> **people were tortured, banished and even executed for carrying infection**

still, dragged off to 'pest houses'; people were
tortured, banished and even executed for carrying
infection; houses and whole villages were burned to
the ground; cities were cordoned off from the outside
world and guarded by military force.

Understandably, many quarantine rules were
broken.

Folk remedies that worked

One of the mainstays of modern disease prevention –
vaccination – was originally learned from the ancient
folk remedies of Africa and Asia.

It had long been obvious that those who
recovered from a disease usually didn't catch it a
second time, yet Western doctors battled helplessly
with disease until the late eighteenth century.
Meanwhile, folk remedies of China, India, North
Africa, Persia and Arabia had been protecting people
against smallpox epidemics for hundreds of years. The
doctor would scrape a knife across the smallpox
pustules of a sick person, then scrape the infected
blade across the skin of a healthy person. Chinese
doctors placed an infected piece of cotton inside one
of the patient's nostrils.

Similar vaccination practices from Turkey were
introduced to England – where smallpox was
dreaded – in 1721; but it wasn't widely used till later
in the century.

Where are you going to, my pretty maid?

English milkmaids were famous for their loveliness. While smallpox raged all around them, scarring and disfiguring the faces of those it struck, milkmaids remained healthy, smooth-skinned and fresh-faced. In 1796, an English doctor noticed that milkmaids who caught cowpox – a disease like smallpox but milder – seemed to be immune to smallpox. In a bold experiment, he developed a fluid from the cowpox blister and injected it into a little boy. Six weeks later he injected pus from a smallpox blister into the same child, and was delighted to report that the boy remained unaffected. After this, vaccination became an accepted way of fighting smallpox and other diseases.

DID YOU KNOW?
The word *quarantine* comes from the Italian word *quaranta*, meaning 'forty'.

Vaccination is based on the idea that introducing safe amounts of germs into a patient will make it produce disease-fighting *antibodies*. These days, dead germs are used, not live ones. If the vaccinated patient later comes in contact with living bacteria of the same kind, the antibodies will be able to fight them off.

DID YOU KNOW?
The word 'vaccine' is based on the Latin word *vacca*, which means 'cow'.

Vaccination is thought to be the best way of preventing epidemic disease.

What Is It?
Syphilis

The room is dark, despite a huge fire blazing on the hearth. A slimy medicine pops and gurgles in a pot hung over the flames. It smells of rotten eggs. The fumes of the brew add to the smell of pus oozing from the sores of the sick people in the room. Some lie moaning on beds, one is sprawled on a pile of straw on the floor, one sweats and drools in a wooden barrel.

Doctors and their attendants move from patient to patient, applying ointment to sores and ulcers, wrapping people in towels, stoking up fires under tubs, measuring the saliva which drools constantly from ulcerated mouths...

It is the early 1500s, and a new disease is raging through Europe and Asia. Capable of turning people's skin into a dripping, lumpy mess within two weeks, the epidemic has touched all classes of people − from beggars to kings. Both King Charles VIII of France and Christopher Columbus have died of it.

According to legend, there was once a shepherd who cursed the sun because a heatwave was killing his flocks. Apollo, the Greek sun god, was offended and punished the shepherd by causing ulcers to break out all over his body. The shepherd's name was Syphilis. He was supposedly the first to suffer from the disease to which he gave his name.

Syphilis is a disease caused by bacteria which are passed from person to person, usually through sexual contact, but also through blood transfusion, broken skin, kissing, and even shared drinking cups.

The first stage of syphilis begins with a small painless blister or ulcer, on the lip, tongue, face, finger, or other point of contact. These ulcers ooze a highly infectious discharge. The syphilis bacteria – called *spirochetes* – travel throughout the bloodstream, and the second stage of the infection appears as a rash. This rash can cover just the hands and feet, or the whole body.

The third stage takes the form of tumors or ulcers which, in the fifteenth century, grew as big as loaves of bread. The ulcers sometimes ate away at the face and throat and created sores down to the bone on the body and limbs. The ulcers seeped pus which smelled so bad that people believed themselves infected by the smell alone.

> **The ulcers sometimes created sores down to the bone**

At this stage, syphilis also begins to eat away at the inner parts of the body – the liver, the heart, the bones, the spinal chord and the brain. Once the spinal chord and brain are infected, insanity follows.

Two famously unpleasant people who owed their madness to syphilis were King Henry VIII of England, and Russia's Ivan the Terrible.

The symptoms of syphilis are no longer as severe as they were five centuries ago. The bacteria have been part of the environment for so long that humans have developed resistance to it. Although a few people still die of syphilis each year, it is now easily combated by penicillin.

3 Curious Cures

All in the Mind

Powdered pearls, ground emeralds and gold dust were once used in medicines. So were live frogs and chicken blood. In fact, the stranger the medicine, the more the patients thought of the doctors who prescribed them.

Doctors knew their medicines didn't always work. However, they also knew that sick people needed something to take their minds off their suffering.

One way to distract patients was to astonish them with outlandish cures. Another way was for the doctor to appear confident and competent – even if he wasn't. According to an old French saying, simply having a doctor present was enough to start the healing process.

The 'bodily humors'

Apart from prescribing frogs and pearls, doctors also put serious effort into the study of disease. For many centuries, they believed that there were certain basic fluids, or 'humors', in the human body. European and Arabic traditions taught that the body contained four *'humors'* – blood, phlegm, black bile and yellow bile. Ayurvedic medicine in India spoke of three 'humors', while Chinese medicine described five.

For continuing health, these 'humors' had to be kept in balance.

Balancing the body

Disease was said to be caused by a lack of balance between the 'humors'. Cures therefore focused on getting rid of the unbalanced humor.

Blood-letting – by opening a vein or applying leeches – was a popular way of reducing fever, said to be the result of too much blood in the system. Metals and poisons, such as *strychnine* and *arsenic*, were fed to patients to help rid them of other excess fluids. According to which 'humor' dominated in the body, doctors gave substances to make their patients either sweat, dribble, urinate, empty their bowels or vomit.

Mercury was popular because it caused extreme dribbling. Dribbling – or salivation – was thought to carry away sickness. Unknown to doctors of the time, however, heavy drooling was not a sign of health, but of mercury poisoning.

For diseases like smallpox, syphilis and bubonic plague, red-hot iron instruments were placed on ulcers, lumps and buboes to 'release the poisons'.

Fowl cures

The eighteenth century was said to be the 'golden age' of fake healers, or '*quacks*'. They often made up their own cures and medicines, drawing on old beliefs, folk traditions, magic – and their imaginations.

For plague, they suggested the patient pluck the tail of a pigeon, chicken or hen, and put the bare tail to the buboe to draw out the poison. If the bird died, the patient was to repeat the process until finally a bird remained alive, meaning that all the poison was gone. For syphilis, one cure was to tie a dead chicken to the ulcers. Other syphilis cures included boiled ant's nest soup and ointments made out of earthworms.

> **boiled ant's nest soup and ointments made out of earthworms**

Abracadabra

In ancient Rome, malaria could be combated by writing '*abracadabra*' on a piece of paper. The paper was then folded and tied around the neck on a piece of cord. After wearing it for nine days, however, the patient had to throw the paper over his or her shoulder into a stream flowing towards the east. If they didn't do this, the cure was useless.

'Abracadabra' was still being used for its magical powers in fourteenth-century Arab countries, and again in seventeenth-century England. People made magic triangles out of the letters, wrote it on charms to wear around their necks, and wrote it on the walls and doors of their houses as a cure for bubonic plague.

Folk medicine

In South-east Asian countries, traditional folk medicines included rice gruel, onions, ginger, fresh tea leaves and guava buds. In Egypt, plague boils were supposedly soothed if a ring made of fresh myrtle was worn on the little finger. In England, a large roasted onion filled with figs and certain herbs would supposedly draw poison from a buboe if left on it for three hours. In many countries, doctors tried to avoid smallpox scars – or pock marks – by wrapping patients in red cloth and putting them in a bed hung with red curtains.

Such cures had the ability to give patients hope and, sometimes, even relief from their sufferings. However, they had no real power against deadly disease.

Holy words, holy water

When doctors and their potions failed to lessen the effects of bubonic plague, Muslims in the Middle East turned to the divine powers of the *Qur'ān* – Islam's holy book. One cure was to recite a particular verse eleven times, spit onto one's body and use the saliva as a salve. Another was to write verses in ink on the inside of a cup, fill it with water, wait for the ink to dissolve, and then drink it. A third was to write verses on a piece of paper, set it alight and inhale the smoke.

Devout Catholics still travel to a place called Lourdes, in France, where they believe the water has miraculous powers.

Quicksilver

Mercury was a popular medicine until the middle of the nineteenth century. As well as being mixed with

WHAT IS IT?
Mercury is a white metal which is liquid at normal temperatures. It is used inside thermometers. Mercury is also called quicksilver.

chalk powder and eaten to cause salivation, it was also used to treat skin diseases; it was mixed with several other ingredients as part of a salve.

Quacksalvers

As a treatment for syphilis, mercury was believed to have no equal. Syphilis cures were often carried out by barbers and quacks. Because of the nature of their work, they became known as 'quacksalvers'.

Their method was to mix an ointment from mercury, pig fat and butter, adding vinegar, myrrh, turpentine and sulphur. Sometimes live frogs, chicken's blood or snake poison were also included. This ointment was rubbed onto the patient's skin, including into the open sores. Then the patient was wrapped in towels or blankets, and put somewhere hot – in a room heated with blazing fires, a sealed wooden tub, or even into an oven. This was repeated

DID YOU KNOW?
The popular fashion for wearing wigs in the 1600s was partly due to the amount of baldness resulting from syphilis and mercury poisoning.

every day for a month, while the attendants carefully measured the amount of spittle that drooled constantly from the long-suffering patient's mouth.

Not surprisingly, mercury 'cures' killed as many as half of those they were meant to heal. Some people died of heart failure, some of dehydration, and many from mercury poisoning. One man is said to have survived 10 mercury treatments, but he died of syphilis in the end.

The bark of barks: a bitter brew

In seventeenth-century South America, a Peruvian Indian once offered a bitter drink to a missionary suffering the chills and fevers of malaria. When the missionary recovered, he learned that the drink was made from the legendary *kina-kina*, or bark of barks. Peruvian Indians discovered the healing qualities of kina-kina by watching sick pumas chewing on the bark of the *myroxylon* tree. The Indians stripped the bark from the tree, soaked it in water, and drank the resulting bitter brew.

'Kina-kina' didn't become well-known among Europeans until the 1630s, when the wife of the Spanish governor of Peru was 'cured' of malaria. Kina-kina – or *cinchona* – was soon adopted as an anti-malarial medicine throughout Spanish America. In Africa, where malaria once killed 40–70 per cent of white settlers, cinchona became indispensable.

Cinchona tasted so vile that many patients couldn't bear to swallow it. Furthermore, no two brews of cinchona were alike. While one piece of bark might make a strong and effective medicine, another of

> **Cinchona tasted so vile that many patients couldn't bear to swallow it.**

the same size would provide no relief at all. In any case, chinchona didn't actually cure malaria, it merely suppressed the symptoms.

This problem was overcome in the 1820s, when two French scientists made *quinine chrystals* from the cinchona drink. Quinine was soon available both as powder and tablets, and remained the standard treatment for malaria for the next century.

Unfortunately, quinine pills tasted as ghastly as cinchona, and a single dose often provoked vomiting. Mrs. Livingstone, wife of the famous British explorer in Africa, died of malaria because she kept vomiting up her quinine pills. Persistent use also caused deafness.

Modern medicine

Various anti-malarial medicines are now available. Some prevent an attack, some quickly relieve the symptoms, while others exterminate the infection altogether.

However, malaria parasites have become immune to some of the drugs designed to kill them. While modern medicine has helped remove the threat of many diseases, new germs keep appearing.

The struggle to cure epidemic illness continues.

What Is It?
AIDS

Lukunya, Tanzania, 1983

Young women crowd around the Ugandan salesman, excited by the arrival of this handsome stranger in their village and clamoring to look at the cloth he is selling. It is the loveliest they have seen for years. One pattern – the 'Juliana' – is particularly beautiful.

The villagers are poor, however, and the girls have no money to spend. In the end, some of the girls agree to trade sex with the salesman in exchange for a length of fabric.

Months pass. Those wearing Juliana *kangas* stand out brightly against the worn and faded clothes of their friends.

Then one of the 'Juliana' girls falls ill. Before long, two more also become sick. They lose their appetites, vomit whenever they try to eat, have steady diarrhea, and are so weak they can no longer walk. All eventually die.

The sickness becomes known as '*Juliana's disease*'.

The villagers suspect the cloth trader. They say he was a witch who had put a violent curse on the Juliana cloth. Magic men perform rituals to ward off the evil, but more and more people fall sick and die. Before long, Juliana's disease has spread from Lukunya to neighboring villages. Adults are wasting away, tormented by fevers and diarrhea; they develop swellings and ulcers, are ravaged by infections which noone can cure.

The Tanzanians blame the Ugandans for the disease. Ugandans, however, are also dying: they blame the Tanzanians.

By 1985, Tanzanian doctors learn that the disease which is killing their patients is killing people in other parts of the world as well. Scientists are calling it *Acquired Immuno-Deficiency Syndrome* – or AIDS.

In the United States and Europe, people point to Africa as the place where AIDS originated. The African countries, however, accuse the Americans of purposely creating the disease in their laboratories. People start coming up with all sorts of theories, blaming first one group of people, and then another.

AIDS is a set of symptoms caused by a virus called the *Human Immuno-Deficiency Virus* – better known as HIV. The tragedy of HIV is that it attacks the human immune system – the very system meant to fight germs and prevent disease.

A person can be infected with HIV and not have AIDS right away: AIDS can take as long as 15 years to develop fully. Over that period of time, however, the body's ability to fight disease gets weaker and weaker. Finally, the immune system fails and the 'syndrome' sets in. This is when other diseases – including tuberculosis and rare cancers – attack the undefended body and eventually kill the AIDS patient.

HIV is very sensitive. It can't survive in the open air, and can be killed with disinfectant. It can be passed directly from person to person, in blood, mothers' milk, sexual fluids and saliva, but only if the virus doesn't first come in contact with the air. HIV can't be caught, for example, from an infected person's sneeze.

At the time of writing, there is no vaccine against HIV. There is also no cure for AIDS. Prevention remains the surest way of halting its spread.

FACT FILE
- By 1996, 28 million people worldwide were said to be infected with HIV. A quarter of these had developed full-blown AIDS.
- 4.5 million adults and 1.3 million children had died of AIDS.
- By the year 2000, as many as 40 million people may be infected with HIV.

4 Laying the Blame

Pointing the Finger

The Italians called syphilis the 'French disease'. The French called it the 'disease of Naples'. In Persia, they blamed the Turks and called it the 'Turkish disease' while in Turkey, syphilis was labeled the 'Christian disease'.

The Portuguese blamed the Spanish; the Hindus of India blamed Europeans; the Russians blamed Poland and the Poles blamed the Germans. Everybody blamed everyone else. People have always been quick to point the finger in times of plague; they are quick to look for scapegoats.

Scapegoats

Scapegoat is the name given to people who are blamed for something they haven't done. Scapegoats tend to belong to obviously different groups of people – people with foreign accents, people with 'odd' clothes or hairstyles, different

> **The poor, the weak and the unpopular are regular targets**

religions, or different colored skin. The poor, the weak and the unpopular are regular targets. Muslims in Spain, Jews in Europe, Chinese in Australia; lepers, grave-diggers, homosexuals, beggars, prostitutes, the disabled – all have been, and some still are, scapegoats and targets of abuse in times of plague.

> **DID YOU KNOW?**
> There was once a Jewish custom where people's sins would be transferred onto a goat. The animal would then be allowed to escape, carrying the sins away with it!
> This was a 'scapegoat'.

The scum of the city

When cholera spread around the world in the early 1800s, it was often those living in crowded and filthy conditions who were the worst affected. In the United States, for example, immigrants crowded into big city slums. Most of them had to live in filthy, leaky buildings – putting up with contaminated water and constant disease.

Nearly half of those who died of cholera in New York were Irish immigrants who lived in these slums. When this information reached the ears of non-Irish Americans, they were outraged. Instead of helping the immigrants by organizing safe water supplies, rich people simply accused the Irish of bringing filthy disease into their clean society – adding that it served the Irish right for being poor!

Willing scapegoat

Marseilles was one of ancient Greece's largest colonies. Like any busy port with visitors from countries far and wide, it suffered regular attacks of plague. When this happened, it was traditional for a poor man to volunteer to be official scapegoat. There was an advantage. The man would live in complete luxury for a full year. At the end of 12 months, however, the volunteer would be dressed in sacred clothes and, in a series of rituals, supposedly have all the evils of the city concentrated onto him. Then, after being chased from the city, the scapegoat would be stoned to death.

In this way, a poor man got a taste of riches and – supposedly – the port of Marseilles was protected from any further attacks of plague!

Self-torturers

The *flagellants* of fourteenth-century Europe were another kind of voluntary scapegoat. A crazed religious group, they felt an obligation to cleanse the world by suffering. The idea was to pacify God and persuade Him to forgive humankind its sins and remove the Black Death from Europe.

The flagellants' favorite instrument was the 'scourge'. Designed for self-torture, a 'scourge' was a kind of whip fitted with three knotted leather strips. Iron spikes were stuck through the knots, the sharp

points protruding a couple of millimetres on either side. Followed everywhere by hysterical crowds, flagellants would go into churches, strip off their clothes and begin lashing themselves with their iron-tipped whips until their bodies ran blood, spattering the walls and floors.

Flagellants roamed in groups and processions, moving from town to town and country to country. These self-torturers became so numerous, and such a nuisance, that town authorities finally banned them. Anyone claiming to be a flagellant risked having his head chopped off.

Not surprisingly, it wasn't long before the flagellants disappeared!

Well-poisoners

Other, and far less willing, scapegoats of the fourteenth century were the Jewish people. Desperate non-Jewish citizens – unable to understand the origin of the Black Death – believed that the cause

> **DID YOU KNOW?**
> In those cities where no Jewish people lived, grave-diggers were blamed for well-poisoning. In Spain, Arabs were the scapegoats.

of plague was poison in the city wells; they thought Jewish people had put the poison there.

Hundreds of thousands of Jews were hunted out of Europe. Those who couldn't escape were tortured and massacred by crazed mobs. Mass burnings became regular events. People were tied to

> **Hundreds of thousands of Jews were hunted out of Europe.**

stakes and burned alive, and Jewish houses were set alight with families still inside. Many Jews set their own homes on fire, burning themselves to death rather than giving their enemies satisfaction. By the time the plague was over, there were hardly any Jewish people left in Central Europe.

Modern scapegoats

In the past, syphilis, cholera and bubonic plague all got people searching for someone to blame. Similar talk still goes on, with AIDS as the new focus. Africans, Haitians, prostitutes, drug users, the CIA, monkeys, 'bad' lifestyles, the World Health Organization and homosexuals have each been accused of single-handedly creating or spreading AIDS. Wrongful accusations, scapegoats and false ideas are still alive and well!

What Is It?
Tuberculosis

Ragged clouds part. The moon shines briefly through. Where all was dark before, a figure can be seen in the shadows, bowed beside a freshly filled grave. Is it a ghost in its white robes with mournful eyes and silent tread? Or is it a grieving girl whose young man – once poetic, handsome and coughing – is now buried here beneath the weeping willow tree?

Graveyard poets

Amongst European poets in the 1800s, it was fashionable to write of tragedy and early death. It was even more fashionable for the poets themselves to be pale, thin and tragic. In fact, many thought that illness and early death were a sign of genius. One man was even told he should become ill, if he wanted to be a better writer.

But the idea that sickness and genius went hand in hand gave little comfort to factory workers of the time. In the smoke-filled, dust-choked cities of Europe, hundreds of thousands of laborers were coughing themselves into early graves.

The blood-specked cough so valued by poets – and so deadly to the poor – was due to a disease called *tuberculosis*. The 1800s were its golden years.

The Industrial Revolution that began in the 1700s brought massive changes to the way things were produced, and also to the health of poor people. The invention of machines and factories brought thousands of country people into the cities with the promise of work – and an early death.

Children as young as five years old worked 12 hours a

factory workers were lucky to live past 20 years of age day for a couple of coins, rarely seeing daylight. Even adults earned barely enough money to buy scraps of food, or to pay rent for a tiny room to sleep in. In the mid-1800s, factory workers were lucky to live past 20 years of age.

But what was hell for the workers was heaven for the germs. The smog-darkened towns and windowless houses kept out sunlight, while foul air and overcrowding in factories made it easy for germs to spread. During the 1800s, seven out of every ten European people were infected with tuberculosis.

The tuberculosis bacterium – or TB – is a weak germ in itself. Healthy people are rarely affected by it, even when it is inhaled. However, stale air, lack of sunlight and crowding create a tuberculosis paradise. Poor people in cities, and those who live in over-full prisons and hospitals, are most at risk.

TB doesn't always attack the lungs. It also breaks down other parts of the body, depending on which organs are the weakest. Native Americans, imprisoned on reservations in the 1800s, had healthy lungs and plenty of fresh air to breathe, but TB attacked their bones and brains. Poverty-stricken Irish people were often seen with huge swellings – or scrofula – around their throats, the result of TB in their glands.

Tuberculosis has been affecting humans for thousands of years, and still exists today. The TB germ itself – called *Mycobacterium tuberculosis* – belongs to a family of germs said to be 300 million years old! In Ancient Greece, TB was the most common and deadly disease known to Hippocrates.

One billion people have died of TB in the last 200 years. The disease still kills two to three million people around the world each year – most noticeably in crowded cities like Manila, Bombay and Nairobi. Poverty, bad diets and dark, crowded dwellings are still to blame.

5 Dirt, Disaster and Disease

All night of 29 December 1170, the body of archbishop Thomas à Beckett lay where he had been murdered – on the floor of Canterbury Cathedral in England. As the body cooled, something strange began to happen. Although the archbishop was dead, there was a simmering of movement beneath his cloak.

Next morning, as funeral preparations began, the weeping onlookers suddenly exploded into bursts of horrified laughter. The archbishop seemed to be boiling over. In a seething, heaving, grey mass, lice in their thousands were crawling out from under his clothes – swarming out of his sleeves, out of his collar, and down across his feet.

Filthy Europeans

Until a century ago, Europeans generally stank. Washing and bathing were frowned upon, even among the rich. Fleas and lice were a normal part of life. People openly picked and squeezed at them, and only princesses were taught to do their scratching in private.

> only princesses were taught to do their scratching in private

We now know that fleas and lice can be carriers of bubonic plague and typhus, but noone back then connected them with disease.

PLAGUE AND PESTILENCE

Wearing the same woolen, lice-infested underclothes sometimes for years on end, people blamed other things for plague and pestilence.

True cowards

As well as flourishing in dirt, germs thrive on disaster and pick on the weak. When disaster strikes, so too does epidemic disease. Disaster can strike in many ways – earthquakes, tidal waves, mud slides, floods and hurricanes. In fact, whenever natural forces destroy the basics of healthy living, germs become a menace. Hunger, thirst, heat, cold and misery weaken people so they are less able to fight off disease.

The 'poor plague'

In Italy during the fourteenth century, villagers and peasants were sometimes so hungry that they gathered weeds from the sides of the road and ate them. Their bread wasn't made of grain, but a mixture of powdered leaves, dirt, hay, flowers, bark, moss and animal guts.

Germs prefer the poor. Those who are poor in wealth are usually also poor in health. When bubonic plague arrived in Italy, it was the poor who were worst affected. In some countries, bubonic plague was called the 'poor plague' and 'beggar's disease'.

The Irish potato famine

In 1845, the Irish peasants grew a bumper crop of potatoes. There would be potatoes for breakfast, lunch and dinner, with some left over for the pigs and chickens, too.

Then the rain set in. The sky hung low, and summer turned into one long damp gloom.

The first sign of trouble was a foul stench drifting from potato fields all over Ireland. Leaves turned purple with a rash of spots, while under the wet soil, potatoes were rotting into blobs of black, stinking slime.

More than half the crop 'melted' into the soil. The next year, potato blight rotted the entire potato crop of Ireland, and again the two years following that.

There was no food for the potato-eating peasants. First they ate seaweed and nettles. Then, in their thousands, they starved to death. Some families lost all hope of survival. They crawled to

They crawled to cemeteries, dug their own graves

cemeteries, dug their own graves, lay down in them and waited. Others crouched in their mud huts, huddling together for warmth in one of the coldest

winters on record. The shivering, starving farmers –
their teeth falling out, their children blinded – paid
little heed to the lice that crawled over them.

Sucking blood and multiplying, creeping and
hopping from one unwashed body to the next, the lice
spread typhus as they went. People's faces swelled
and turned black in a rash of spots. Soaring fevers
and delirium sent them into a coma. It was the lucky
ones who died.

Wings of disaster

South Africa, 1748. A black wall stretches along 50
miles of coastline, 3 feet high, gleaming and rotting in
the sun. It is made up of billions of locusts that have
been washed ashore on the incoming tide. The stench
is overwhelming.

A few days earlier, the same wall of corpses was
the biggest swarm of locusts ever recorded. It had
blocked out the sun over an area of 1930 square
miles before being blown out to sea.

Locust swarms aren't always blown out to sea.
Sometimes the wind carries them across fertile
farmlands, with
devastating effects.
People still live in
terror of the massive
whirring which signals
an approaching swarm. Turning the sky dark, they
move like the wrathful hand of God across the
helpless countryside.

> People still live in terror of the massive whirring which signals an approaching swarm.

Pastures which were lush and thriving become
desolate wastelands within hours. The locusts leave
nothing but bare dirt and skeleton trees.

Nineteenth-century illustration of the Great Plague of London, 1665

Fumes as a form of disinfectant; a newspaper man being fumigated before going to report on a cholera outbreak

Opposite page top: A World War II theater slide warning of the danger of dengue fever

Opposite page bottom: Three doctors visiting a smallpox patient. Smallpox is now considered an extinct disease

As dangerous as an enemy bomber -

MOSQUITOES CARRYING
DENGUE FEVER
can Cripple an Army ...disorganise a Community

THIS MOSQUITO BREEDS ONLY IN AND AROUND HOUSES

(1) SCREEN ALL TANKS OR APPLY KEROSENE TO WATER SURFACES
(2) DESTROY ALL BOTTLES, TINS & OTHER THINGS WHICH HOLD WATER
(3) EMPTY ALL BUCKETS, VASES, ETC. AT LEAST EVERY WEEK.

Drs. Girdlestone, Wilson, & Plummer visiting the patient

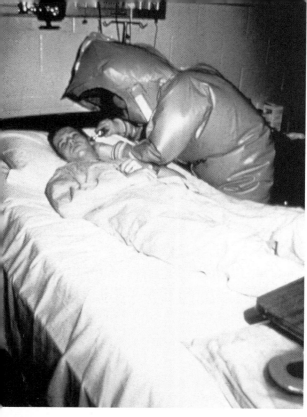

Treating an Ebola
patient in Atlanta,
1995. The Ebola virus
is one of the deadliest
known today

Below: Hospital
workers carrying the
coffin of a nun who
died during the Ebola
outbreak in Kikwit,
Zaire, 1995.

In the past, locusts were often blamed for the epidemics that followed. However, locusts didn't create disease. They simply provided a disaster which allowed illness to take hold. Starving, homeless and desperate people have weakened *immune systems* – their bodies can't fight off germs.

Famine and sickness have always gone hand in hand.

What Is It?
Typhus

Eastern Europe, 1812

To the Polish peasants, Napoleon's Grand Army was not a welcome sight. Crossing the River Niemen from Prussia on its way to capture Moscow, the force totaled nearly half a million soldiers and horses. The Grand Army would soon strip the landscape bare.

The French soldiers were equally displeased. These peasants lived in starkest poverty. They had little to eat, tiny amounts of dirty water, and ramshackle huts made filthy by the animals they lived with. The army chose to camp out in the open rather than take over the flea-infested hovels.

Their aim was to avoid filth and disease. However, they hadn't counted on their own lack of hygiene. With barely enough water to sip on, they never washed – despite marching all day beneath a blazing sun. Food shortages and bitterly cold nights added to their hardships.

Lumbering its way across the unwelcoming Polish countryside, the army gradually weakened. Hunger, thirst, dirt and lice prevailed. Sleeping soldiers huddled together – both for warmth and in case of attack during the night. The stage was set for the deadliest battle of all. Before long, typhus was raging through Napoleon's army.

Typhus is caused by pathogens – or germs – called *rickettsia*, which are passed to humans from lice. The fever shoots up suddenly, even while the patient's body shakes with chills. Severe pains torture the arms and legs. After a few days the rash breaks out, accompanied by agonizing headaches. The spots begin like tiny, pink flea bites, soon changing to purple and then to brown. Not everyone dies of typhus, but in the weakened Grand Army, young men died quickly in huge numbers.

Napoleon's campaign to extend his Empire into Russia became famous – both for its stupidity, and for the horrors endured by his soldiers. Within a month of entering Poland, 20,000 horses had died of thirst, and 80,000 men had been struck down with typhus. Even so, Napoleon insisted on marching towards Moscow.

Even after the battle of Smolensk – which, combined with repeated waves of typhus, had shrunk the force from over half a million to only 130,000 – he pressed eastwards. The road to Moscow was strewn with French corpses.

The French took Moscow in September 1812. However, the Russians had left little to take. Before fleeing the city, they set it alight and destroyed food supplies. With nowhere to live, nothing to eat and no hospitals, the invaders died in droves. Defeated by disease and starvation, 95,000 French soldiers left Moscow a month later.

The retreat from Moscow was even more disastrous. The remaining soldiers struggled with icy mud and wretched roads; they were harassed by Russians from behind, and plagued by the ever-present epidemic. Only 25,000 made it back into Poland. There, forced to eat leather – and even each other – many men starved before freezing to death in the bitterly cold winter. The greatest slayer of all, however, remained the enemy within – typhus.

Of Napoleon's original 500,000, only 1000 soldiers recovered from the campaign.

6 The Germ and the General

Germs have been responsible for the deaths of more soldiers than the combined wars of all the kings and generals of history put together. Foot soldiers dropped in their tracks, cavaliers and officers toppled from their horses, and tents were full of dead and dying men. Armies turned their backs on each other, burning their tents and desperately retreating from disease.

Mighty microbes

Disease has helped bring down some of the greatest civilizations of history. It was mosquitoes and malaria – not enemy invasions – which weakened the ancient Greeks and Romans. Both started out warlike and confident, conquering their neighbors and expanding their borders with unrivaled vigor and bravery. However, both also brought malaria back with them from their foreign wars.

At home, they created breeding places for mosquitoes by stripping forests and allowing farmland to become swampy. Rulers and citizens of both empires ended up depressed, lazy and undecided. They became easy targets for their enemies.

> **DID YOU KNOW?**
> Some of the signs of malaria are depression, weariness and lack of interest.

The Greek Empire was vanquished by the Romans. Rome, in turn, was overcome by the barbarians. However, it may be that neither Greece nor Rome would have fallen if they hadn't first been weakened by disease.

Antoninan and Justinian Plagues

While malaria sapped the strength of Rome, two other plagues stormed through a sagging empire to deliver the deathblow. An unknown disease – called the Plague of Antoninus – started in 165 A.D. and raged for 14 years. It killed so many people that cities and villages were left empty, farming and business came to a standstill, and warplans had to be abandoned.

PLAGUE AND PESTILENCE

The last blow for Rome, however, came in 541 A.D., during the rule of Emperor Justinian. A

(**killing 10,000 people a day**)

ferocious pandemic of bubonic plague roared through the eastern Empire, shredding the entire population and killing 10,000 people a day in the Byzantine capital of Constantinople. In 10 years, successive sweeps of plague had reduced the eastern Empire to less than half of its original population.

By 570 A.D., invaders from the north had conquered most of Italy. The Roman Empire had collapsed.

History is full of examples of how generals have been defeated by germs.

Fifth century Attila the Hun was set back in his campaign to take over Europe by famine and by a mysterious disease which cut through his mobs.

Eleventh century Famine and disease destroyed the First Crusade so rapidly that there wasn't time to bury the dead.

Thirteenth century An epidemic swept through an invading French army in Spain. It killed many men, most officers and finally the king. The remaining soldiers had little choice but to turn around and leave.

Fifteenth century Spain had ongoing wars with the Moors. In one battle, the Moors killed 3000 Spanish soldiers. However, typhus then proceeded to attack the Spanish force, killing over 11,000.

Sixteenth century A French army besieged the Italian city of Naples. Just when it seemed that the starving

Italians would have to give up, typhus suddenly broke out in the French camp. In only one month, 25,000 men died. When the remainder of the French force tried to sneak away one wet night, they were chased and cut to pieces by the freed citizens of Naples.

Again and again, microbes have affected the outcome of wars. Historians often wonder how history would have looked if germs hadn't had such a hand in shaping it.

STARTLING STATISTICS OF THE NINETEENTH CENTURY

The Crimean War (1854–56)   Just over 63,000 men died of battle wounds. During the same period, 104,000 men died of disease – mainly typhus.

The American Civil War (1861–65)   Of the one million men who fought in this war, twice as many were killed by disease as killed in battle. The Federal armies lost 93,443 men from war wounds, while 186,216 died of disease.

The Boer War, South Africa (1899–1902)   Over 6000 men died in battle over two years. In the same period, more than 11,000 soldiers died of disease.

World War I

By the beginning of the twentieth century, people had begun to understand the origins of disease. It was also recognized that disease was more deadly than enemy gunfire.

| disease was more deadly than enemy gunfire |

As a result, a great deal of energy was spent keeping both the Austrian and German troops free of lice. However, typhus thrived in the armies and cities of Eastern Europe, where hundreds of thousands died of it during the war. Typhus also remained alive and well in prison camps.

DID YOU KNOW?
Another disease carried by lice – called 'trench fever' – was common amongst all armies during World War I. It was related to typhus, but wasn't a deadly illness.

Germs as well as shells and bullets could be received from enemy forces. World War I was held up for six months in 1914 while a disease-free Austrian army hung back, more afraid of typhus raging among the enemy Serbian troops than of the Serbians themselves. Austrian leaders knew that risking an epidemic meant risking victory.

In the footsteps of war

The combined effects of German invasions and revolution had devastating effects on the Russian people. In 1918 health services were in a mess, people were homeless, and the worst famine in thirty years had left countless people starving.

Accompanied by cholera, typhoid and dysentery, the worst typhus epidemic in all history struck Russia. It lasted for four years and affected between 20 and 30 million people. As many as three million people died of the disease. The epidemic was so devastating that politicians feared it would undo all the work they had done in patching up the war-shattered country.

Cleaning up the troops

By the time World War II was under way in 1939, armies had become far cleaner. Both sides knew that wars had once been won and lost through the interference of typhus. All soldiers were vaccinated against a wide range of diseases, and cleanliness was drilled into them as part of their training. A newly discovered insecticide called DDT was used to dust down whole armies, killing nits and lice and wiping out the threat of disease.

> **DID YOU KNOW?**
> DDT stands for dichloro-diphenyl-trichloroethane. It is now considered a deadly poison, and is illegal in most countries.

Lice and cruelty

However, no such health precautions were taken inside the Nazi concentration camps. These 'death camps' were set up by German Nazis as prisons for Jews and other unwanted people. They were packed into unheated shelters without blankets or running water, treated to daily doses of cruelty and terror, and so badly fed that they lived in a state of famine. These inhuman conditions were highly favorable to lice.

Of 45,000 prisoners in Belsen camp, for example, 20,000 suffered typhus in a three-month period. The remainder had tuberculosis or dysentery. When the British army freed Belsen inmates in April 1945, they found thousands of corpses lying side by side with the sick and the dying. Beyond either help or hope, 13,000 more died soon after liberation.

Beyond either help or hope

Germ warfare

After World War II, many countries developed 'bombs' which were full of deadly germs. The idea was to drop them on enemy countries and kill the citizens with epidemic disease. Some people say that as many as 25 nations are developing this kind of biological weaponry.

> **DID YOU KNOW?**
> In the 1700s, British settlers in America gave unwashed blankets from smallpox hospitals to unsuspecting Native Americans.

What Is It? Smallpox

First to be affected were the rugged Arawaks on Haiti. Then the Calusa of Cuba, followed by the Mexican Aztecs. Then disease spread from Mexico, south to Peru and the Mayas of Yucatan, the Guatemalan highlanders, the Incan Empire of the Sun, and the Amazon. Fanning in all directions like a deadly grassfire, it spread north, to Florida and up the mighty Mississippi, then outwards throughout the whole of what is now Canada and the United States.

One after another, whole nations crumpled. In less than a century, 90 per cent of Native Americans – both north and south – had died. Only the invaders thrived – the Spanish, the Portuguese, the French. And smallpox.

Smallpox arrived in the New World by sailing ship in the early 1500s. Traveling faster than the Europeans who brought it, the epidemic raced ahead of the invaders, spreading from its entry point in Haiti to every corner of the American continent – from the Aleutian Islands near Russia in the far north, to Tierra del Fuego on the southernmost tip of South America.

The empires of Central and South America had astonished the new arrivals. At the beginning of the 1500s, no European city – not even London or Rome – could match Tenochtitlan, the Aztec capital, and there were twice as many people living in the Americas as there were in all of Europe.

By the mid-1600s, however, this was no longer true.

Compared with Europeans of the time, Native Americans were unusually healthy. They washed themselves daily and had smooth skin – unlike the pock-marked Spaniards. They had straight white teeth – unlike the worn, discolored or missing teeth of the Europeans; they smelled sweet – unlike the Spanish, who doused themselves in perfume to hide their odor; and they lived to the ripe old age of 50 – unlike the invaders, who were lucky to survive 30. Furthermore, they were almost disease-free.

Until, that is, the arrival of smallpox.

Being so free from disease, Native Americans were also more vulnerable to it. They had none of the immunities that protected the Europeans. When smallpox hit them, it hit hard.

Called the *Orthopoxvirus*, the smallpox germ is now said to be extinct. However, it was once very common and highly contagious. One drop of moisture from the mouth of an infected person could be deadly. It caused chills and fevers, and stinking, oozing sores on face and body. The sores were sometimes so painful that patients would scream in agony every time they tried to move. Survivors were left with ugly scars and some were blinded.

Amongst the once-mighty empires of Central America, only one in 10 people pulled through to discover this for themselves. Of the 25 million Aztecs at the beginning of the 1500s, only two million were left half a century later.

7 Picking Up the Pieces

The sky hasn't changed. The sun still rises in the east. The trees are the same, and breezes rustle the leaves. Water continues to flow between riverbanks, and to fall from the clouds as rain.
Yet everything is different.

Cemeteries sprawl larger than towns. Houses stand empty. Scrub grows where tilled fields once lay in neat rows. Silence competes with scavenging dogs in deserted market squares and weeds grow through the stones on temple steps.

Grim heritage

Epidemics have long arms. The effect of a single outbreak can span whole continents and resonate down through the centuries. Plagues have won wars, carried out mass slaughter, toppled empires and stamped out civilizations. But despite massive wipe-outs, life goes on. How do epidemics affect those who survive – those left picking up the pieces?

DID YOU KNOW?
Most of the major forests in Europe date back to the Middle Ages. They sprouted after bubonic plague emptied the countryside of farmers, and fields reafforested themselves. Before bubonic plague, Europe was in danger of becoming a treeless waste.

Where have all the people gone?

Farm animals in Indonesia starved to death when the great influenza pandemic of 1918 passed through. There were no people to take them to fresh pasture. Orphaned children, crying in their houses, were left to die because there was noone to come to their rescue.

> **the only areas of growth were cemeteries**

In Egypt, so many peasants died or fled their homes during the Black Death that the countryside became a desert. Waterwheels stopped turning, gardens and irrigation canals dried out, orchards shriveled. In Cairo, the only areas of growth were cemeteries. Wealthy suburbs became ruins or slums, and royal gardens turned into dust and rubble. Market squares and mosques stood empty while once-busy roads blurred back into the ground.

> **DID YOU KNOW?**
> So few farm workers were left in Palestine after the Great Mortality that Muslim rulers and their household servants had to go into the fields to collect the harvest themselves.

In plague-struck Medieval Europe, some children were left with no known relatives. Orphaned girls from rich families were often tricked into marriage by men who wanted their money. It happened so often that laws were made forbidding it.

> **They slept on beds and ate off plates for the first time in their lives.**

Poor people moved into unclaimed houses. They slept on beds and ate off plates for the first

> **DID YOU KNOW?**
> In Norfolk, England, villages emptied by plague in the Middle Ages remained deserted for the next 600 years.

time in their lives. Families who had never owned anything took over abandoned farms, mills and even mansions, becoming as wealthy and powerful as they had once been downtrodden and poor.

Power to the peasants!

In medieval times, peasants were regarded as little better than farm animals. They existed only to work. They didn't ask questions, and they never made demands.

The Black Death changed all that.

It killed off so many peasants that there weren't enough workers to go around. European landlords, used to 'owning' the peasants who tilled their fields and harvested their crops, suddenly found they had lost both their workforce and their power over it. If they refused to pay good

> **Unemployed people were... branded on the forehead**

wages, the peasants now simply walked away to find better pay elsewhere. It was something that had never happened before.

Rulers struggled to control the situation. In England, laws were passed which made it illegal to leave a job. It became a crime to demand higher pay. People caught receiving – or even paying – higher wages were put in prison. Unemployed people were labeled as outlaws and, if caught, branded on the forehead with a red-hot iron.

Despite tougher and tougher laws, the peasants refused to obey. Plague had made them both rare and valuable.

Far-reaching effects

In a few decades, smallpox destroyed the ancient empires of America (see pages 59–60). The Spanish, Portuguese, Dutch and French invaders of the New World ended up with vast territories, but noone to rule and noone to work for them. They had to look elsewhere for replacements. Their gaze fell on Africa.

> **DID YOU KNOW?**
> The Aztecs, Mayans and Incas called smallpox the 'Great Fire' and the 'Easy Death'.

Filling the empty spaces

Africans were kidnapped from their homelands and herded onto Portuguese slave ships. They were so closely packed that they couldn't move for the entire journey. Chained to the spot, they were forced to sit in their own – and everyone else's – bodily wastes. Thousands died of disease and many ships were little more than floating cemeteries. Those who survived the slave ships brought fresh germs with them.

As many as 14 million Africans were eventually

> **many ships were little more than floating cemeteries**

> **DID YOU KNOW?**
> The slave ships left a stinking trail of floating raw sewage behind them on the ocean, which could be smelled long after the ship had passed over the horizon.

transported to the New World. The slavers didn't realize they were also bringing unknown tropical diseases with them across the Atlantic – malaria and yellow fever were soon creating major health problems.

Travel diary of a pandemic

Yunnan Province, China, 1855

The land 'beyond the clouds' was home to a demon the world had tried to forget. But in isolated Yunnan – where China backed against the Himalayan Mountains – bubonic plague still existed, underground.

The people of Yunnan had always been careful to avoid contact with rats that carried the dreaded disease. But in 1855, a rebellion by native Yunnans brought Chinese troops across the Salween River and ways of life which kept rats and humans apart were disrupted. The balance between people and plague was upset. Meanwhile, refugees streamed out of Yunnan. Unknown to the world, *Yersinia pestis* had once again been unleashed.

Hong Kong, 1894

In 1894, bubonic plague erupted in the cities of Hong Kong and Guangzhou. Hong Kong was a major trading city, and junks and steamships crammed its busy harbor, leaving daily for distant countries. Hidden in the cargoes, black rats accompanied the ships wherever they went. So did *Yersinia pestis*.

The Pacific Rim, 1894–99

Carrying plague, ships sailed from Hong Kong to Japan, Manchuria and Russia. Across the Pacific Ocean, plague was transported to Honolulu and the United States. Traveling south, it entered Singapore, Burma, Vietnam, Malaysia, the Philippines and Indonesia.

Bombay, 1896

To the west, plague arrived in Bombay, India, and spread inland from village to village with the crowds who fled the epidemic. In India, a million people were soon being infected every year and, at the height of the disaster, over a million died of it in one year alone.

The Middle East and Africa, 1899

After steaming through the Arabian Sea, plague arrived at the Arabian peninsula and toured Mecca, Medina and Jeddah with Muslim pilgrims. From Arabia, it traveled into Egypt and North Africa, later sailing around the Mediterranean to stop off at ports along the way. Plague also disembarked at the Persian Gulf and took to camel caravans, trekking overland into Turkey, Persia and Russia.

Sailing from Bombay across the Indian Ocean, plague went to Africa. It landed in cities on the east coast and transferred to rail, traveling inland to settle permanently among rodents living around the shores of Lake Victoria.

PLAGUE AND PESTILENCE

South America, 1900

Having circled Africa, the tireless traveler sailed across the Atlantic Ocean to visit South and Central America. On arrival in Brazil it switched from ocean to river steamer, chugging up tropical waterways into the heart of Paraguay and Argentina. Where the rivers stopped, plague transferred to steamtrains, going onward by rail to all major inland towns. It eventually made its way to the United States.

Australia, 1901

Bubonic plague sparked major panic in Sydney when it jumped ship in Darling Harbor and visited the nearby slums. In spite of massive clean-ups, inoculations and rat hunts, 535 people died of plague in Australia.

Mission accomplished, 1902

By 1902, *Yersinia pestis* had circled the globe. In every major seaport of the world, plague now began to spread in earnest. Six years of pandemic followed.

The worst was over by 1908, but bubonic plague wasn't finally defeated until the 1920s. By that time, 10 million people had died worldwide.

8 Germs on the Move

In the past, germs traveled the world slowly – no faster than a person could walk, a horse could gallop or a boat could sail. With the invention of faster transport, germs traveled faster as well. Some of the world's deadliest diseases are now no further than a plane trip away.

Germs need to stay on the move to survive. They need to get from person to person, from crowd to crowd, from country to country. With neither wings nor feet of their own, germs rely on the wings and feet of others.

> **DID YOU KNOW?**
> Deadly cholera bacteria can live for months floating around in algae on the ocean's surface.

Flying into Europe

In 1347, bubonic plague was catapulted into Europe. The Mongolian Empire was expanding westward, and its army had already laid siege to the city of Caffa on the Black Sea – a vital trade link between Europe and Asia – when its soldiers were suddenly struck by plague.

Instead of burying the dead, the Mongolians loaded them onto catapults and hurled them over the city walls to land among the citizens of Caffa.

The people inside the city were forced to handle the corpses that

> the corpses that came flying into their midst

came flying into their midst. It wasn't long before they fell ill as well. Only a few months later, the Black Death was rampaging throughout Europe and the Middle East.

Stranger danger

In tropical Africa, ancient customs once prevented people from transmitting disease. When they traded, people from one village laid their goods on the ground at an agreed spot. Then they backed away. People from the other village then came forward and put down goods of similar value, before also drawing back.

When both sides agreed to the trade, they each picked up their new belongings and left the area – without once having spoken or been close to one another.

Before the European invasion of tropical Africa, Africans obeyed strict rules. They frowned on change, and were suspicious of strangers. Each region had its own diseases. People living within those regions had developed their own immunities. By keeping to their tribal areas, Africans kept their germs to themselves.

Germs on foot

Walking is the slowest form of transport. Even so, travel by foot has played a major role in the spread of disease. When animals and people walk about, insects and germs go with them.

In fourteenth-century Europe, people flocked out of cities to escape the plague. In nineteenth-century Asia, citizens flooded into the countryside to escape cholera. In twentieth-century Africa, people fled their villages to escape the terrifying Ebola virus.

fleeing crowds carried the germs with them

Instead of avoiding disease, these fleeing crowds carried the germs with them. They spread the epidemics across the countryside as they went.

Breaking the germ barrier in Africa

In the fifteenth century, Portuguese explorers stopped along the coast of Africa to kidnap people for slavery. The growing slave trade soon brought Africans out of their villages. Some traded in slaves themselves, others were forced to enter foreign territory to escape the slavers. The boundaries which once kept people and diseases apart were broken.

Over the next four centuries, Europeans invaded all parts of Africa. They forced huge numbers of

Africans to work for them. Thousands of men were taken to work in mines and on plantations far from their homelands.

As these masses of people moved out of their traditional areas, they ran into diseases never experienced before. At the same time, they walked their own germs across borders, introducing them to others.

Epidemic disease – once unknown in Africa – soon became commonplace.

Germs under sail

The Portuguese and English transported diseases as well as slaves across the oceans. Before the arrival of African slaves in the Americas, malaria was unknown in the New World. Yellow fever was unknown anywhere except in tropical Africa. Both diseases soon became major killers in America, killing Native Americans and European settlers alike.

WHAT IS IT?

Yellow fever, like malaria, is carried by mosquitoes. Infected mosquito larvae probably traveled in water barrels aboard slave ships. Symptoms are headache and terrible pains in the body, followed by vomiting of greasy, black blood. The disease is called yellow fever because the victim's skin usually turns yellow.

When the Mongolians catapulted Caffa with plague in the 1340s, the Italian merchants who lived there fled, taking the plague with them. Many died on their way home across the Mediterranean.

DID YOU KNOW?

Lisbon and London were famous in the fifteenth century for the diseases that raged whenever ships came back from the tropics.

People in the ports of Italy refused to let the 'death ships' enter, some towns even firing burning arrows at them – driving away their returning citizens as if they were enemies. Despite their efforts, bubonic plague soon landed in Italy.

Ghost ships

In 1349, a strangely silent ship drifted into the harbor of Bergen on the west coast of Norway. Its sails flapped and sagged, its ropes dangled loosely. Not a soul was visible on board.

Ghost ships like this once haunted the coasts of Europe, the Middle East and North Africa – floating about the Mediterranean without a crew. Drifting with the tides and lurching aimlessly with the waves, they eventually broke to pieces against the shore or sank. It was sheer bad luck that this one had entered a harbor.

The ghost ship of Bergen had a cargo of wool. It was also loaded with dead men, dead rats, and deadly fleas.

Bubonic plague had arrived in Scandinavia – by sea.

Separate collections

Two thousand years ago, the Old World was made up of four civilizations: one in China, one around the Mediterranean Sea, one on the sub-continent of India, and one in the Middle East. Each civilization had its own collection of germs. Rugged mountains and impassable deserts kept these collections apart.

Then traders found ways of linking the civilizations. Chinese merchants would trek across the highlands of Xinjiang in China's north-west, then cross the deserts and grassy plains of Central Asia before arriving at the Black Sea.

> **DID YOU KNOW?**
> A *caravan* was a large group of merchants traveling together, often using horses, camels and mules to carry their merchandise.

Traders from both east and west were soon following this route back and forth between Asia and Europe – traveling in caravans and exchanging luxuries such as silk, spices and furs.

The traders were also exchanging deadly disease.

Germs on the hoof

Other travelers joined the slow-moving caravans as they moved through different countries. It was one of the safest ways to travel, since the caravans were protected by armed guards.

> **Armed guards…were no protection against black rats or disease.**

Armed guards, however, were no protection against black rats or disease.

> **DID YOU KNOW?**
> Many of the epidemics afflicting the last years of the Roman Empire were brought by traders from the Far East.

Hitching rides with the pack-animals, black rats were carried away from their native Central Asian homes. Along with rats, bubonic plague soon found its way to the wider world – riding on the backs of horses and camels.

Germs on the loose

In October 1976, Mayinga – a young Zaïrean nurse – developed a severe backache. This was soon followed by blinding headache and stomach pains. Although she didn't admit it, Mayinga knew what the matter was.

Mayinga was one of the nurses caring for a Catholic nun who had died from Ebola fever. Now she herself was coming down with the disease. For two days she pretended it wasn't happening. Instead of reporting her symptoms, Mayinga caught a taxi into Kinshasa, the capital of Zaïre. She went about the city, catching cabs, waiting in crowded rooms, standing in long lines, and visiting two hospitals to seek relief for her headache and increasingly red eyes. Mayinga came into close contact with at least 37 people.

At last – unable to bear her pain and fear any longer – Mayinga went back to the hospital where she worked. She admitted herself with suspected Ebola fever and was isolated in a private room.

WHAT IS IT?
Ebola fever is caused by one of the newly discovered *filoviruses*. It strikes suddenly, and causes high fevers, blood poisoning, vomiting of blood, severe diarrhoea and bleeding from all body openings – including the eyes, the nose, around the teeth and through the pores of the skin. Victims suffer horribly and their body fluids are highly contagious. Ebola fever kills 90 per cent of those it infects. Another, only slightly less deadly, filovirus is called Marburg. It is also found in Africa.

PLAGUE AND PESTILENCE

Despite every kind of care and treatment, however, Mayinga died.

Germs on the wing

Meanwhile, panic spread like wildfire. News that someone with Ebola fever had been mixing with people in crowded Kinshasa put the whole world on alert. If any of those who had been in close contact with Mayinga boarded a plane, the dreaded virus could possibly spread to all major centers of the world.

Germs can travel halfway

> **Germs can travel halfway around the globe in less than 24 hours.**

around the globe in less than 24 hours. They 'hitch rides' with airline passengers, some of whom don't even know they are infected. In the meantime, these people pass their germs to many others.

> **DID YOU KNOW?**
> By 1990, 280 million people were travelling internationally by plane every year.

Despite Mayinga's wanderings, no other Ebola cases appeared in Kinshasa. The world had been spared an Ebola pandemic – for the time being.

What Is It?
Influenza

Iowa, 1918

The nights are getting longer, evenings are turning cold and leaves are starting to drop from the trees. The Iowa Cedar Rapids Swine Show is over, and porkers are returning to their barns. All over the state, however, pigs are coming down with the flu. They are sneezing, coughing, staggering and dying in their thousands.

Elsewhere, bison, sheep, moose and elk are also suffering. So are humans.

In Spain, people fell sick early in 1918. At the same time, American soldiers, waiting in camps to be transported to the war in Europe, were also falling ill and dying. So were French and British soldiers in Europe, and a rapidly increasing number of civilians.

Before the year was over this flu epidemic – popularly known as 'Spanish Lady' – had spread around the world and was killing millions.

Only two other pandemics in recorded history killed more people worldwide than the Great Influenza Pandemic. The Justinian Plague (page 54) killed over 100 million, the Black Death (pages 11–12) killed 62 million, and the 1918–19 flu about 21 million.

Like all bouts of flu, this particular type started with headaches, fevers, sore muscles and a dry cough. But unlike other outbreaks, this strain came on suddenly, spread like wildfire and killed even strong and healthy young people within three to five days.

PLAGUE AND PESTILENCE

It also allowed other killer bugs to move into the lungs, the brain and the blood. People's lungs turned into frothing jelly, they bled through the nose, their skins turned blue, and they choked to death on their own mucus.

The most remarkable thing about the 1918 pandemic was that it wasn't only grandparents and babies who died of it, it was those in their teens, their twenties and thirties – people with strong immune systems who should have recovered within a few days.

People who went to work in the morning feeling only a little tired, arrived at their destination dying. Many were carried dead off public transportation, having boarded in full health.

Scientists aren't sure exactly where the killer flu of 1918 came from. Some think it grew on a pig farm in the United States. Others say it evolved from the European battlefields of World War I. Most agree it was an unusual twist of nature.

They also agree it could happen again.

9 Germs That Twist and Jump

In 1987, people living around Lake Baikal in Siberia were astonished to find thousands of dead seals washed up along the shores. As many as 20,000 dead seals were eventually counted – nearly 70 per cent of the lake's seal population. When scientists were asked to investigate, they discovered the seals had died from a disease usually found only in dogs.

> **DID YOU KNOW?**
> When epidemics spread through different species of animals, they are called *panzootics* (pan-zo-otics).

The year before, an epidemic of distemper had spread among Siberian sled dogs. Owners threw their dead dogs into the lake, and the virus, which since ancient times had affected only dogs, 'jumped' species to the seals, nearly wiping them out.

Germs jumping in farmyards

Influenza is an ancient bird disease. Water birds, especially ducks, regularly pass their germs on to other birds and animals, contaminating ponds and troughs with their infected droppings.

On farms, where ducks and and other animals live closely together, flu germs pass most easily between ducks and pigs. Farmyards, therefore, are good breeding grounds for new flu viruses.

PLAGUE AND PESTILENCE

> **DID YOU KNOW?**
> In the eighteenth and nineteenth centuries, horses and cows usually became ill before an outbreak of flu among humans. A flu pandemic in 1889 began as an epidemic of coughing among Russian horses.

Influenza probably jumped from animals to humans over 2000 years ago, when people first started farming pigs and ducks in China. Farm workers all over the world have been exposed to influenza ever since.

Mystery illness

Early each morning in San Joaquin – a Bolivian village near the headwaters of the Amazon River – the women get up in the pre-dawn to prepare food for their families. One of their early chores is to sweep the dirt floors of their huts. The dust still hangs thick in the air when the families sit down to breakfast.

In the 1960s, people of San Joaquin started coming down with a mysterious disease. They developed chills and fevers, headaches, muscular pains and convulsions. Their skin would seem to turn black as thousands of tiny blood vessels burst and leaked. Three out of every ten affected people died of either convulsions or heart failure.

Deadly dust

Scientists were brought in from the United States to analyze the problem. While researching the possible causes, four of them mysteriously caught the disease too. They recovered, but a volunteer assistant was not so lucky. His colleagues noted how his hand had been bitten – and then urinated on – by an angry mouse, but it wasn't until over a year of painstaking research that the team found the cause of the illness – mouse urine!

While the villagers of San Joaquin slept, field mice raided their food stores and fed on crumbs. Everywhere they went they left patches of urine.

In the morning, when the women swept, clouds of dust, dried urine – and germs – were thrown into the air. Household members then breathed in the contaminated dust and became infected.

> **DID YOU KNOW?**
> Germs which jump from animals to humans are called *zoonoses*.

When a mouse eradication campaign was set up in the village, the epidemic disappeared.

Modern zoonoses

The virus killing people in San Joaquin was named Machupo fever, after a nearby river. It belongs to a group of newly discovered germs called *arenaviruses*. These viruses are carried by mice, rats and bats.

Several other new germs have also recently appeared – many of them associated with rodents or bats. Although these diseases may have existed for thousands of years, changes in the environment have brought the animals which carry the germs into closer contact with humans.

Zoonoses of history

Germs have been jumping from animals to humans for the last 10,000 years. *Anthrax* is an ancient disease which mainly kills cattle, but which also affects horses, sheep and goats. *Glanders* – a disease of horses – has been passed on to people for at least two and a half thousand years. Cats have been passing parasites to their owners since the ancient Egyptians brought them into their homes, and

rabies has been passed from mad dogs to people for over 3000 years. *Brucellosis* – a disease passed on through goats milk – was a common disease in ancient Greece, while *measles* is thought to have come from dogs.

Mutating microbes

Although many plagues have been mentioned in ancient writings, some of them may no longer exist.

Bacteria, viruses and parasites are in a constant state of *evolution* and change. For example, when flu germs jump between ducks and pigs, they change slightly – or *mutate* – with each jump. In this way, it doesn't take long for new strains of influenza to evolve.

Antibiotic-resistant bacteria

As they change and adapt, many microbes also become resistant to medicine. Some bacteria, for example, are no longer vulnerable to antibiotics. In 1952, a bacteria called *Staphylococcus* was treated successfully with the anti-bacterial drug penicillin. Thirty years later, *Staphylococcus* had changed so much that less than 10 per cent of all *Staph.* infections could be treated with penicillin.

> **DID YOU KNOW?**
> Through the use of antibiotics, humans have created germs which never existed before in nature.

By 1993, the drug Vancomycin was the only definite killer of *Staphylococcus*. In 1996, bacteria emerged which were resistant to every known type of medicine.

> **DID YOU KNOW?**
> Bacteria that live and breed in hospitals can live in detergent and on bars of soap.

Vancomycin, the strongest antibiotic drug available, is now finding it increasingly hard to combat bacteria which cause cholera, tuberculosis and typhoid.

Combining bacteria

When bacteria evolve, they don't simply become resistant to drugs, they also combine with other types

of bacteria to produce whole new breeds of germs –
sometimes stronger and deadlier than either of their
'parent' bacteria.

Until 1992 there were two types of cholera in
the world – classic cholera and El Tor. Classic
cholera was the more deadly of the two, but El Tor
had the ability to survive for long periods of time
while floating around on the ocean.

In December 1992 a new type of cholera
emerged. It is as deadly as classic cholera, and it has
the survival stamina of El Tor. In other words, it is
more dangerous than either of them.

Virus fear

In the 1980s, a mild disease of snowshoe hares in
Russia suddenly caused a serious epidemic among
humans. Two virus types – neither of them harmful –
had combined to create a
deadly disease.

> **DID YOU KNOW?**
> The visna virus is a
> disease similar to HIV,
> which affects sheep. It
> spreads through flocks
> when the sheep cough on
> each other.

Before 1970, HIV was
a fairly harmless virus. Then
something happened that
sparked a sudden mutation.
Since then, HIV has mutated
at a rate of 1 per cent every
year; by 1995, there were at
least six distinct types of HIV.

One of scientists' greatest fears is that HIV will
evolve until one day it becomes an air-borne virus. It
would then spread as easily as the flu.

What Is It?
Lyme disease

Deer graze peacefully in the glades. Chipmunks pause in their scampering while squirrels dart headlong down the birch trunks. Ferns grow among the shady undergrowth.

The woodland paradise, however, is not all it seems to be.

Although it has been a wildlife preserve for nearly 100 years, the idyllic scenery is a newly created environment – a regrowth woodland resulting from a century of heavy logging.

Where deer graze calmly, there were once wolves, wild cats and bears. Where shrubs crowd together, there were towering oaks and larches. Where undergrowth blocks the path there were deep shadows of open forest floor.

A new, scrubby version has taken the place of the old forest. Deer abound. So do raccoons, chipmunks, mice – and ticks. In the shady, wooded areas of the US east coast a new disease is flourishing.

In the mid-1970s, a number of people in the town of Old Lyme, Connecticut, came down with a similar sickness. Many of the victims were children, who had spent their summer vacation playing in woodland surrounding their suburban homes.

It wasn't the flu – although it felt like it. Nor was it rheumatoid arthritis – although it felt like that, too. Victims had fever, headaches, sore throats, nausea, fatigue, swollen glands, stiff necks and aching muscles. While some of them recovered quickly, others got worse and stayed that way.

Doctors called it Lyme disease.

The cause was eventually discovered in 1982. Bacteria

called *Borrelia burgdorferi* were being passed from white-footed mice to ticks, who in turn passed them on to campers, hikers and playing children who brushed against tick-infested shrubs, bushes and undergrowth.

Although the ticks preferred deer, the presence of people in their environment had given them an alternative.

Lyme disease is now the most frequent sickness caused by insect bite in Europe and the United States. About 10,000 new cases are reported every year in the US, and there were 20 times as many cases in 1992 as there were 10 years earlier. Cases have been found in Australia, Japan, China and South America.

Lyme disease appeared among humans due to changes people made to the environment. The changes were part of an attempt to heal and reafforest the countryside, but the new forests had a different balance – one which allowed white-footed mice and their ticks to multiply in a way they had never done before.

The modern woodlands also had suburbs nestled among them. Germs and humans had been brought closer together, and the result was an epidemic which seemed to spring from nowhere.

10 Nature Out of Balance

Where floods and droughts once ruled the farming calendar, there is now a steady supply of water. Where a mighty river once rampaged after the rains, there is now a controlled flow all year round. The changeable and unruly River Nile in Egypt has been tamed.

The Aswan High Dam was built across the Nile in 1970. The water it held created Lake Nasser – a huge stretch of water 254 miles long which reaches from south-eastern Egypt across the border into Sudan.

Nature rearranged

The dam changed the ecology of the Nile River – slowing its flow, putting an end to yearly flooding and submerging 1,976,843 acres of land. This new system

---

WHAT IS IT?

Schistosomiasis is caused by parasitic worms which cause a wide range of illnesses in humans. People get the worms from working or playing in contaminated water. Larvae pass through the skin, enter the bloodstream and make their way to the inner organs where they grow into worms. There they cause all sorts of disease, from mild fatigue to heart disease and cancer. Schistosomiasis infects about 200 million people in Africa, Asia and South America.

---

was good for farming.

It was also good for snails.

Snails play an important part in the breeding cycle of parasites called *schistosomes*. Untroubled by the seasonal floods and droughts which once kept them under control, both snails and schistosomes could now breed without interruption. There was a sudden and dramatic increase in *schistosomiasis*.

Double trouble

While locals battled with increased schistosomiasis, an unknown and even deadlier epidemic arrived, infecting 200,000 people around Aswan. Hundreds of them died, along with thousands of cows and sheep. Rift Valley fever – once confined to Kenya, thousands of miles to the south – had moved into Egypt.

WHAT IS IT?
Before 1977, Rift Valley fever was a livestock disease. It caused epidemics among farm animals, but never people. Rift Valley fever is passed on by mosquitoes.

Carried by the wind, mosquitoes from Kenya and Sudan had drifted into the Aswan region, finding a perfect breeding place in the newly created Lake Nasser. Disease-bearing mosquitoes were soon breeding there in their countless millions.

DID YOU KNOW?
Rift Valley fever broke out again in Aswan in the early 1990s. Similar dam related epidemics have erupted in other developing countries.

Controlling nature

Ever since the beginning of history, people have tried to control nature. Clearing forests for farms, driving a parasite to extinction, damming the Nile, taking antibiotics, taming cats and cows, and installing air-conditioners are all ways in which people try to control the natural world.

However, when natural systems are altered, unexpected side-effects can occur. Some side-effects are worse than others. Most side-effects are irreversible.

The transformation of wild countryside into farmland sometimes means that humans are put into closer contact with nature than is healthy for them. Some agricultural practices have released new germs from their natural hiding places.

> **Some agricultural practices have released new germs from their natural hiding places.**

In from the wilds

The Argentinian *pampas* (grasslands) are home to a rare type of field mouse. These field mice are, in turn, host to a rare type of disease. Left to themselves, the mice and their disease don't affect humans. In contact with humans, however, they can prove deadly.

During World War II, many countries turned to Argentina for supplies of beef and corn. In order to meet increasing demands, Argentinian farmers began ploughing into the previously untouched *pampas*. These huge expanses of grassy, treeless plain seemed ideal for farming.

PLAGUE AND PESTILENCE

Flushed out of their native grasslands, the mice moved into the cornfields where they found food in abundance. It wasn't long before their numbers swelled. The field mouse, once so rare, was soon the most common rodent in the region.

In the late 1940s, a horrible disease started killing Argentinian farm workers. It mainly affected those who worked the harvesting machines. No one could work out why.

A decade later, investigators discovered that field mice were the culprits. Like the mice of San Joaquin, they carried a deadly and previously unknown arenavirus. They called the Argentinian disease Junín fever.

WHAT ARE THEY?

Arenaviruses are a group of viruses carried in the excreta of bats, rats and mice. They cause hemorrhagic fevers, which involve disrupted capillaries, internal bleeding and shock. Victims can bleed to death, die from heart attack or from major convulsions.

Thriving on grasses that grew among the cornstalks, the mice left their droppings all over the crops. When harvest time came, the machinery churned up clouds of dust filled with the virus. The machines also crushed the mice themselves, adding sprays of infected blood to the dust which the workers were breathing.

Mission impossible

In 1954, the World Health Organization launched an ambitious project. It set out to wipe malaria from the

WHAT IS IT?
Legionnaire's disease is a sickness caused by the invention of air-conditioning. *Legionella* bacteria are now one of the main causes of pneumonia in hospitals.

face of the planet. Malaria-carrying mosquitoes were to be made extinct and the ancient disease was to disappear for ever.

Armed with the powerful poison DDT, world authorities set out on a massive spraying spree. Scientists were convinced that within a decade, not only malaria, but all insect-carried diseases would vanish. Major universities were so confident that they cut the study of malaria from their courses.

> Scientists were convinced that... all insect-carried diseases would vanish.

Success seemed to be just around the corner. European countries and the United States were sprayed so heavily with DDT that malaria was almost non-existent by the early 1950s. Ten years later, Sri Lanka had only 18 cases of malaria, compared to one million in 1955.

Then things started to go wrong.

As countries used more and more poisonous sprays to combat insects, *DDT-resistant* mosquitoes began to appear. At the same time, *chloroqine-resistant* malaria turned up in countries as far apart as Thailand and Brazil.

By 1975, noone was mentioning malaria eradication. Not only were mosquitoes immune to DDT, but the malaria plasmodium itself was becoming tolerant to more and more of the medicines meant to control it. Scientists were beginning to realize that making sweeping changes to nature can result in unforeseen disaster.

In some parts of the world, the malaria problem was worse than ever.

DID YOU KNOW?

In 1975, there were over twice as many people suffering from malaria as there had been during the malaria eradication scheme. Cases of the disease in India increased by 230 per cent, and in China by 900 per cent.

Success story

Ali Maow Maalin, of Somalia, is famous. On 26 October 1977, he was said to be the last person on the planet to have smallpox. From that time on, smallpox was declared extinct. Unlike malaria, smallpox was defeated.

The smallpox eradication campaign had taken 10 years of effort. It was carried out by 150,000 health workers who gave 250 million vaccinations a year across more than forty countries! The workers braved civil wars, jungles, deserts, mountains, floods, guns and murderers in their struggle to vaccinate every human being on earth.

The smallpox germ — the *orthopoxvirus* — now exists only in a few frozen test tubes. They are kept under heavy guard in research centers in Atlanta, and in Moscow, Russia. However, although the eradication of smallpox was successful it is now seen by many scientists as a lucky but freakish event.

> **DID YOU KNOW?**
> Fourteen diseases, once thought to be under control, are now becoming widespread again. they include pneumonic plague, tuberculosis and cholera.

Crowd control

When people stop dying of disease, populations skyrocket. Countrysides which once supported a couple of million people are suddenly required to feed several million.

> **DID YOU KNOW?**
> Under the grip of malaria, Sri Lanka had a population of about 10 million people. When malaria eradication cut the island's death rate by half, the population started swelling. By 1994 the population was nearly double.

PLAGUE AND PESTILENCE

The side-effects of overpopulation are many. It forces people to cut into untouched forests, or to plough wild grasslands, for farming. It forces them to hunt and eat animals that aren't a usual part of their diet, exposing them to dangerous animal germs.

DID YOU KNOW?

In 1994, people crowding into the refugee camps and prisons of war-torn Somalia and Rwanda suffered horrible epidemics of cholera. Yellow fever, typhus, typhoid, pneumonia and dysentery continue to attack warring countries.

Overpopulation also invites epidemic diseases as water and food supplies break down. It sparks civil war, as people battle for the right to more land. War, in turn, invites further disease. Scientists are beginning to realize – in some cases too late – that humans can't expect to rearrange nature without sparking unforeseen events. From the extermination of germs, to the pollution of oceans, human actions ripple through the ecosystem – for years, decades and even centuries.

> **Overpopulation also invites epidemic diseases**

Further Reading

For upper primary and lower secondary readers

The Black Death
by James Day
Wayland, Hove, East Sussex, 1989

Natural Disasters: Famine, Drought and Plagues
by Jane Walker
Gloucester Press, London, 1992

For advanced readers and adults

A Field Guide to Germs
by Wayne Biddle
Allen & Unwin, Sydney, 1995

Plague's Progress
by Arno Karlen
Indigo, London, 1996

The Fourth Horseman: A Short History of Epidemics, Plagues and other Scourges
by Andrew Nikiforuk
Phoenix, London, 1993

Rats, Lice and History: A Study in Biography
by Hans Zinsser
Little, Brown, Boston 1963

Index